Stop Smoking

Useful Guidelines And Professional Insight For Overcoming Dependence And Embracing A Smoke-Free Lifestyle

(Strategies For Cessation Of Nicotine Dependence And Achieving A Smoke-free Lifestyle)

Timothy Nichols

TABLE OF CONTENT

What Is The Efficacy Of Respiratory Exercises? 1

Personal Experience 6

Being Aware Of Nicotine Addiction 18

Practical Strategies And Counsels For Cessation Of Smoking 22

The Real Reasons Why Nicotine Gums And Patches Don't Work 28

What Is Nrt 52

How To Quit Smoking 81

Formulating A Strategic Roadmap Employing The Four-Step Pilt Methodology 103

Foundational Principles For Transforming Ingrained Patterns Of Behavior. 133

What Is The Efficacy Of Respiratory Exercises?

Indeed, aerobic exercises aid in enhancing cardiovascular wellness, while respiratory exercises enhance pulmonary efficiency.

Pulmonologists, who are esteemed specialists in the field of respiratory problems,

I recommend proposing respiratory exercises to individuals who suffer from COPD and asthma, as they aid in maintaining optimal lung health.

It is advisable that an individual engage in these activities when they perceive their lung capacity to be optimal in order to enhance endurance and continue with the regimen even if they experience shortness of breath.

Deep breathing exercises can potentially facilitate the enhancement of lung capacity. As an illustration, according to The English Lung Establishment, the practice of deep breathing can aid in the elimination of accumulated pulmonary secretions that may result from pneumonia, thereby facilitating better pulmonary ventilation.

To execute this activity, commence by taking deep inhalations, approximately 5-10 times, following which one must proceed to cough a few times before repeating the process.

16

Various activities, such as the application of compressed lip breathing, can aid in the management of attentiveness in individuals facing respiratory illness. As indicated by the Public Establishment for Wellbeing and Care Greatness, this may assist with shortness of breath brought about by Coronavirus.

However, it should be noted that medical experts have yet to conduct a thorough examination regarding the effects of respiratory exercises on pulmonary function in individuals afflicted with the Coronavirus.

Currently, there exists no evidence to suggest that they serve as a viable or efficacious means of managing symptoms associated with this novel condition.

17

In general, it is advisable to consult with a medical professional prior to attempting any novel respiratory techniques.

While engaging in respiratory exercises may confer benefits to...

individuals

gentle

respiratory

Instances wherein individuals exhibit severe symptoms may necessitate the administration of oxygen therapy or the implementation of a mechanical ventilator.

Individuals experiencing respiratory symptoms of concern are advised to seek consultation with a healthcare professional.

Chapter 6

Conclusion

Implementing techniques such as compressed lip breathing and stomach L-breathing can effectively facilitate the enhancement of an individual's pulmonary function.

Regardless, it is advisable to seek consultation from a certified healthcare professional prior to attempting any novel exercise regimen, including respiratory exercises. This holds particularly true for individuals who have underlying medical conditions, such as COPD.

Personal Experience

Upon having ceased smoking four years ago, I never retrospectively considered resuming the habit.

I intend to elucidate to you the manner in which I have accomplished it.

If one wishes to quit smoking, drinking, or any other habit, one must modify their perspective towards said habit.

Per your knowledge, it is imperative to note that smoking can have a detrimental impact on an individual's well-being, elevating the likelihood of cancer.

Although the gradual depletion of your health may not immediately prove fatal, it poses a potential risk of progressing towards mortality, which warrants immediate attention and remedial measures.

It was within my sole discretion to undertake the task; no external influence was compelling me to do so. I subsequently comprehended that insofar as the action was self-inflicted, the authority to desist lay within my purview. Generally speaking, the matter is uncomplicated, yet frequently, we assume a posture of helplessness amidst a situation which does not exert complete control over us. we are harming ourselves.

On that very day, I decidedly relinquished my smoking habit and consequently embarked on a short jog for a block, nearly succumbing to exhaustion. I accomplished this objective by substituting my detrimental smoking habit with the healthy practice of running.

I was unwell, experiencing nausea and dizziness. It is intriguing to contemplate in hindsight, however, during that period, I experienced uneasiness, illness, and such a feeble state that I was not able to run even for a short distance. Nevertheless, my unwavering determination propelled me to take action, and thus, the subsequent day, I ventured outdoors and jogged for two city blocks. Despite being unwell and experiencing nausea, I persevered with my run and ultimately completed a distance of two and a half kilometers. What proved advantageous to me was substituting an adverse dependency with a beneficial one. As an illustration, should you aspire to cease smoking, consider substituting it with an alternative activity, such as engaging in a game, partaking in swimming, engaging

I would like to refrain from making any personal judgments, but it would be highly advisable for you to exert all possible efforts to gain control over these matters.

I empathize with the sentiment of being persistently urged by multiple individuals to abandon a pursuit, despite their inability to effectively influence your cognizance and assist you in arriving at a judicious determination. Nevertheless, rest assured that your resolute perseverance shall remain unwavering.

It can be inferred that refraining from smoking and drinking may be conducive to augmenting one's capacity to economize. Demonstrate to those who doubt your abilities that you possess the aptitude to accomplish the task, invalidate the perspectives of your peers who hold the belief that you lack the necessary capabilities, and abstain from the consumption of alcoholic beverages entirely. It can be asserted that individuals hold the power to dictate the course of their lives, and as such, they are capable of achieving this feat. Let us, therefore, rally behind one another and beseech divine intervention to surmount this addiction.

Triumphing over the cycle of detrimental patterns and dependency.

Kindly do not hesitate to recite this prayer, my esteemed companions. Assume a position of prayerful submission and beseech your divine maker with heartfelt supplication. If all attempts to conquer addiction have proven futile, it is time to implore intervention from a higher power.

I withhold any form of criticism or unfavorable evaluation towards you; rather, I feel affectionate towards you.

Nevertheless, to witness the efficacy of this prayer, it is imperative that you exhibit genuine contrition. I am not insinuating that you harbor maleficent intentions, however, the psychoactive agents you consume possess profound metaphysical connotations and therapeutic intervention alone may not suffice to absolve you from their influence. Instead, you need deliverance. It has come to our attention that certain individuals might have encountered instances of self-stimulation, same-sex relationships, and erotic materials through domestic aides, associates, or other kin; however, we must remind you that such immoral behaviors are deceitful manifestations instigated by malevolent forces.

We are eliminating all obstacles hindering the attainment of desired outcomes. I solemnly proclaim, "O Lord Jesus, I acknowledge your divine identity as the begotten Son of God; and I firmly believe in your boundless love for me, demonstrated by your excruciating death for the expiation of my transgressions." Today, I affirm that you are the sovereign ruler of my life and the only means of my salvation. Furthermore, I embrace everlasting life with gratitude, beseeching deliverance from all adverse afflictions that have afflicted my corporeal existence hitherto. At this moment, I am invoking a miracle.

As I address the audience through the guidance and influence of the Holy Spirit, I extend my hands towards the binding spirit of various addictive patterns and behaviors that have enslaved you, fostering an insatiable and undesirable impulse within. Through my prayer in the name of Jesus, I command this spirit to depart immediately. Furthermore, I interpose a spiritual barrier between you and any human agent that seeks to sponsor or enable such behavior, whether it be smoking, drinking, or any other detrimental habit. In this manner, I beseech that you remain distant from such a deleterious lifestyle permanently, akin to the metaphorical gulf that separated the rich man and Lazarus. I hereby renounce any and all soul ties resulting from any connections, and in the name of Jesus, sever them immediately. Any portion of your destiny that has suffered on account of this, is hereby released by order of the Almighty God. I declare that your transgressions have been absolved and the adversary shall not have any power to leverage your past against you. You are now reborn in Christ and a new being altogether, in the name of Jesus.

Being Aware Of Nicotine Addiction

What is Nicotine Addiction?

Nicotine is present in all tobacco-containing products and regrettably, the propensity to acquire addiction to this specific compound is exceedingly effortless. Upon the onset of smoking, typically during the adolescent years, one may find that after having consumed a few cigarettes within a matter of days, their nicotine tolerance begins to develop.

But why is it that nicotine is that addictive?

It is noteworthy that nicotine has the capacity to stimulate the release of chemical substances that activate the reward pathway in the brain.

If one engages in consistent use of cigarettes and other tobacco-containing products, the neurochemical reward pathway in the body undergoes corresponding adjustments. Subsequently, one develops a conditioned response to seek tobacco as a means of gratifying their urge for nicotine, despite their acute cognizance of the repercussions accompanying prolonged smoking habits and their sincere desire to discontinue this practice. The yearnings that you experience for smoking will serve as a reminder to increase your nicotine consumption levels to alleviate the stress and discomfort typically associated with nicotine withdrawal symptoms. The aforementioned withdrawal symptoms typically commence within a few hours, owing to the rapid action of nicotine. If one refrains from smoking a cigarette, it is typical to experience symptoms of nicotine withdrawal, such as intense cravings, difficulty concentrating, irritability, anxiety, restlessness, insomnia, and low affect. As a smoker, one elevates their nicotine levels by consistently smoking throughout the day, a practice that is commonly observed among the majority of smokers.

What measures can be taken to effectively address nicotine addiction?

Upon cessation of smoking, one may experience symptoms of nicotine withdrawal. However, there is positive news to be anticipated. Nicotine withdrawal symptoms typically reach their zenith around the third or fourth day, as per the majority of smokers, while also finding that such symptoms usually cease within a period of no more than 10 to 14 days. The variation may vary among individuals.

Despite any lack of immediate sensation, it is a factual matter that one's health shall improve progressively. In as little as a fortnight, one's physiological state can be substantially free of the discomforts conventionally linked to nicotine deprivation. Upon this occurrence, your inclination towards smoking is anticipated to decrease, thereby facilitating a smoother transition towards a smoke-free lifestyle. It is atypical for individuals who smoke to undergo a plethora of symptoms for a prolonged duration.

The second notable aspect lies in the fact that the aforementioned symptoms can be effectively mitigated through the utilization of NRT, or otherwise known as nicotine replacement therapy, or any other prescribed medication which specifically targets smoking cessation.

Practical Strategies And Counsels For Cessation Of Smoking

In addition to the aforementioned 4-Step System for smoking cessation, the following catalogue of ten alternative and efficacious techniques are available to individuals seeking to quit smoking:

1. Kindly apprise those in your immediate vicinity of your intentions to cease tobacco consumption. Individuals who engage in smoking behavior require the support and mentorship of their loved ones in order to achieve long-term success in their cessation efforts. This may have a potential impact on certain members of the family or acquaintances who may also indulge in smoking, thereby motivating them to consider quitting as well.

2. Please eliminate any items present in your residence that may serve as a reminder of smoking. Objects such as ashtrays, cigarettes, and lighters easily make aspiring quitters yearn for a hit.

3. Maintain a consistent record of your advancement by keeping a journal. This initiative will furnish smokers with a daily log that can be readily examined to ascertain potential areas for further enhancements, thereby optimizing their non-smoking endeavors.

4. It is imperative to stay vigilant about the indications of nicotine withdrawal which may manifest during the initial weeks and months of smoking cessation. Individuals who smoke should anticipate experiencing symptoms including heightened anxiety, fluctuations in mood, alterations in eating patterns, and sleep disturbances

during the initial phase of abstaining from smoking. It is advisable that they also make preparations for suitable treatments to mitigate the withdrawal symptoms that they are likely to encounter.

5. Maintain an optimistic outlook. Terminating one's efforts can be an arduous task. Adversities are prevalent; nonetheless, it is imperative to persevere and retain self-confidence in surmounting the habit of smoking. The adoption of optimistic perspective is tantamount to achieving favorable outcomes.

6. Engage in physical activity or engage in fitness training. An inherent outcome of smoking cessation is an elevated propensity towards greater food intake, as nicotine withdrawal tends to stimulate a larger appetite

among smokers. Engaging in physical activities on a regular basis in conjunction with a well-structured nutritional regimen are imperative steps towards achieving weight reduction.

7. Don't hesitate to request assistance when needed. Frequently, individuals who smoke experience a sense of inadequacy and fear social repercussions of revealing their inability to adhere to cessation efforts. These circumstances should not prevail. Medical practitioners, specialized healthcare professionals, communal support networks, close acquaintances, and fellow tobacco users will consistently be available to lend an ear and offer assistance.

8. It is recommended to consume a significant amount of water throughout the day. This removes nicotine and other

toxic chemicals in the body acquired from smoking.

9. It is advisable to strongly consider incorporating daily sessions of deep breathing exercises into your routine. Engaging in this activity for a minimum duration of five minutes would prove to be considerably beneficial in managing smoking-related urges. Taking deep breaths facilitates the ability to maintain focus amid the onset of cravings.

10. Consistently maintain a state of inspiration and motivation within yourself. One may achieve this by constantly reinforcing in one's mind the long-term advantages of quitting and the significant individuals in their life who would be pleased with their endeavor to cease smoking.

The Real Reasons Why Nicotine Gums And Patches Don't Work

The most frequently recommended and widely utilized alternatives for smoking are nicotine patches and gums. Both remedies are constituent elements of Nicotine replacement therapy, employed to mitigate the urge to smoke.

Although alternative nicotine sources have gained popularity, it cannot be guaranteed that they will prompt smokers to quit their unhealthy habit. While it may be initially efficacious in the initial stages of cessation, in the long term, it does not effectively facilitate complete cessation for an individual. The majority of individuals who utilize nicotine patches and gum have a tendency to relapse to smoking after a few months due to a reported sense of monotony with these substitutes. Their principal action is limited to preventing the manifestation of withdrawal symptoms during the initial weeks and months of discontinuation. Furthermore, it should be noted that the aforementioned NRT products are comparatively expensive if compared to cigarettes, thereby discouraging smokers from persistently using or even contemplating purchasing them.

Nicotine replacement therapy represents a transitory approach to a apparently enduring issue. Hence, it is paramount to deliberate upon and implement a methodical approach by embracing various alternative remedies in tandem.

Chapter 8

Would you prefer this to be for our benefit or for the benefit of others?

"I shall endeavor to discover a means,

Otherwise, I will fabricate one."

Philip Sidney

When we undertake a course of action in our lives, it is typically motivated by a desire to fulfill our personal goals, aspirations, and necessities. Alternatively, our actions may be driven by an obligation to fulfill the expectations placed upon us by others. This principle is of a general nature and has wide-ranging relevance to numerous facets of your life, which is distinctly evident.

On occasion, the shared interests of both parties coincide, whereby there appears to be an overlap or convergence between our own interests and those of another individual. In actuality, there exists a predominant interest that prevails over others.

For instance, in the event that we determine to shed weight and reinstate our slim figure; we can embark on this journey for two distinct purposes: benefiting our personal health and enhancing our physical appearance, or we can do so to appease a loved one, or comply with counsel from a healthcare professional or specialist.

There are those who are inclined to undertake a task with greater dedication when it is intended for personal gain, while others possess a greater sense of commitment when the task accomplishes the desires of another individual. Acquiring an understanding of this particular behavior would greatly aid in identifying the most compelling rationales for quitting smoking. If an individual is driven by personal satisfaction, they may identify compelling reasons such as an improvement in their overall well-being, heightened self-worth, increased confidence, financial savings, and the gratification of receiving a reward upon the accomplishment of their goal. Conversely, if one is inclined to fulfill the desires of others, they may seek motivation to quit smoking through reasons such as the benefit it would bring to their spouse or partner.

You may consider the encouragement of your loved ones, or the pursuit of proving skeptics wrong, as potential motivating factors. Alternatively, seeking professional medical advice with regards to the specific health hazards of smoking may also aid in making an informed decision.

If one is uncertain regarding their predominant source of motivation, it may be beneficial to compile a list of motivations stemming from both categories in order to yield a more conclusive outcome. It is imperative that one identifies the appropriate motivations that will provide sustenance throughout the journey towards achieving their objectives, as they serve as a crucial aid in surmounting challenging moments. Create a catalog of compelling reasons, ranging from five to ten, for abstaining from smoking, inscribe them on a parchment, keep it with you, and peruse the document periodically and consistently. During the initial days, it is advisable to peruse the list on multiple occasions in a day until its contents are firmly ingrained in your memory. Subsequently, it would be advantageous for you to reiterate your incentive either audibly or internally whilst queuing, immobilized at traffic signals, awaiting a person or object, or during moments of stasis. Throughout the day, one can avail several opportunities to utilize their free time efficiently.

Continuously reiterate your justifications for resuming the act of breathing. This will accelerate your drive towards accomplishing your objective. When one possesses sound justifications, it can act as an impetus or an ignited force that propels them towards their objective. Identify the appropriate motivational factors for ceasing smoking. If you carefully scrutinize your motives and find them to be convincing, you shall experience an overwhelming surge of inspiration, an indomitable fervor that shall impel you towards accomplishing your desired objective. In the event that the aforementioned situation did not occur, it would be prudent to endeavor to modify or alter one's motivation until it reaches its optimal level and serves as a catalyst for enhanced performance. Thoroughly peruse and revisit your motives to foster a surge of vitality. Given the profound level of motivation you are currently exhibiting, let us address the apprehension towards change.

CHAPTER EIGHT

Following the release of the primary report by the Surgeon General's Advisory Committee on Smoking and Health in 1964, over 20 million premature deaths have occurred in the United States as a result of cigarette smoking. Despite measures undertaken in the United States to reduce cigarette smoking among adults from 42% in 1964 to 14% as of 2019, the current number of smoking adults still surpasses 34 million individuals. Moreover, the consumption of some tobacco product is estimated to be utilized by 50.6 million adults in the United States, equivalent to 20.8% of the populace.

The utilization of cigarette smoking, including secondhand smoke exposure, stands as the foremost cause of preventable diseases and mortality within the United States. It is paramount to note that in excess of 480,000 deaths transpire annually as a result of such use. If the current rate of cigarette consumption continues, a staggering 5.6 million children under the age of 18, residing within the United States, are expected to perish from ailments stemming from smoking.

The act of smoking cigarettes has been proven to have a causal relationship with the development of various illnesses affecting practically all organs of the human body, leading to an increased risk of coronary heart disease, stroke, chronic obstructive pulmonary disease (COPD), diabetes mellitus, and lung cancer. The most common cause of lung cancer can be traced back to smoking. Additionally, cigarette smoking can cause complications in pregnancy, harm the developing fetus, and have a negative impact on overall health. Studies indicate that smokers may lose more than a decade of life expectancy. However, the risk of mortality for smokers who refrain from smoking drastically reduces with the cessation of the habit, with the risk of mortality decreasing significantly the earlier they quit smoking. To be specific, quitting smoking at the age of 40 years or below can remove over 90 percent of excess mortality caused by prolonged smoking.

Breathing in handed-down cigarette smoke is additionally negative to wellbeing. It constitutes a blend of gases and minute fragments encompassing smoke derived from the combustion of tobacco products, in conjunction with exhaled smoke. This smoke is replete with an extensive range of chemicals, comprising hundreds of noxious substances, 70 of which are carcinogenic in nature.

Exposure to secondhand cigarette smoke can lead to the development of several tumors as well as respiratory and cardiovascular illnesses. It can also pose serious health risks during pregnancy and for infants and children. In fact, exposure to secondhand cigarette smoke during pregnancy can result in a range of adverse outcomes for unborn babies and infants. Such outcomes may include premature birth, low birth weight, stillbirth, sudden infant death syndrome (SIDS), lower respiratory infections, asthma, and middle ear infections.

Nicotine, an inherent component of tobacco, possesses a remarkably addictive quality. It has been suggested that tobacco industries deliberately modify their products to foster and maintain addiction.

Although cigarette smoking remains the predominant form of tobacco consumption in the United States, other tobacco products are frequently employed by and targeted towards specific racial, ethnic, and economically disadvantaged populations, as well as children and young adults. Examples of such products include but are not limited to bidis, hookah/waterpipe tobacco, snus, dissolvable tobacco, cigars, cigarillos, electronic nicotine delivery systems (ENDS), and electronic cigarettes (also referred to as e-cigarettes).

Electronic cigarettes and Electronic Nicotine Delivery Systems (ENDS) are devices powered by batteries. They consist of cartridges filled with nicotine or containers that allow for the addition of nicotine-containing liquid or "juice." These devices emit a vapor that is inhaled as a mist containing flavorings, varying levels of nicotine, and other toxic substances. Manufacturers and advertisers promote e-cigarettes as a less expensive and safer alternative to traditional cigarettes, despite numerous studies linking e-cigarette use to harmful effects, including increased blood nicotine levels, physical symptoms, and adverse impacts on indoor air quality. An alarming concern is the increased focus on e-cigarette use as a smoking cessation method by manufacturers, advertisers, and retailers. The American Academy of Family Physicians (AAFP) does not endorse ENDS as smoking cessation devices in any population due to insufficient evidence of their effectiveness. The AAFP supports the seven tobacco cessation options approved by the U.S. Food and Drug Administration (FDA), recognizing that pharmacotherapy and counseling significantly improve cessation outcomes.

Source of inspiration

The American Academy of Family Physicians respectfully implores all public and private institutions involved in tobacco cessation and prevention programs to enhance and focus their initiatives. It's crucial to implement robust initiatives to mitigate the harm caused by the consumption of tobacco and nicotine. The AAFP supports the objectives of the American Academy of Pediatrics, American Cancer Society Cancer Action Network, American Heart Association, American Lung Association, Americans for Nonsmokers' Rights, Campaign for Tobacco-Free Kids, and Legacy® who advocate for governmental action to achieve the following three robust objectives15:

Reduce the prevalence of smoking to less than 10% by the year 2024.

Protect the health and well-being of all individuals in the United States by preventing exposure to secondhand cigarette smoke.

Eliminate the mortality and morbidity resulting from the usage of tobacco.

Family physicians can proactively advocate for tobacco and nicotine control measures at various levels, including local, state, and public, thereby contributing to positive health outcomes. Family physicians are trusted members of their communities and can serve as effective advocates in collaborating and advocating for policy reform, particularly at the local level. In order to achieve these robust objectives, the AAFP requests support in the areas delineated below.

Advocacy at the local and state levels for:

Tobacco control measures founded on evidence-based strategies, such as the implementation of augmented tobacco excise levies.

Comprehensive tobacco control programs supported by revenue generated from taxation.

In the absence of tobacco products within pharmacies and medical facilities, and the cessation of all forms of tobacco transactions in said establishments.

Comprehensive methods for enhancing indoor air quality that involve the utilization of electronic cigarettes and electronic nicotine delivery systems (ENDS).

Comprehensive protection coverage is offered without any additional co-payments or shared costs, encompassing Medicaid coverage, for evidence-based cessation counseling, medications, and over-the-counter tobacco cessation remedies.

Enhanced accessibility of tobacco cessation services for all patients, irrespective of their healthcare coverage.

The FDA's Center for Tobacco Products (CTP) has instituted a stringent and timely policy regarding all products containing nicotine.

A study is being conducted on e-cigarettes to examine their health effects, durability, and effectiveness as a possible cessation device.

Restriction of accessibility and proliferation of electronic cigarettes among minors and adolescents.

By means of these various undertakings and initiatives, the AAFP, in collaboration with its sections and distinguished members, is poised to act cohesively towards mitigating the scourge of tobacco-related mortality and morbidity.

Family Physicians' Role

The impact of American tobacco use behavior can be significantly influenced by the actions of family physicians. Approximately 70% of individuals who utilize tobacco products seek medical attention on an annual basis. Recent empirical evidence corroborates the affirmative influence that primary care physicians can impart by promoting smoking cessation amongst their patients.

It is imperative that patients refrain from smoking. Nearly 70% of adults who engage in the practice of smoking attest to the need to discontinue, and more than half have attempted to quit within the past year. However, a mere fraction of them - less than 33% - have endeavored to terminate their habit through scientifically-proven cessation techniques. It is worth noting that quitting smoking can be an arduous undertaking that requires external support. According to a particular inquiry, a mere percentage of 3 to 5 of adult individuals who endeavored to quit smoking without availing any external assistance managed to maintain their abstinence from smoking for a period of 6-12 months.

Although many individuals endeavor to quit smoking independently without engaging in cessation programs, researched evidence indicates that evidence-based quitting programs could enhance success rates twofold. Moreover, if medical practitioners were to educate ninety percent of smokers about the benefits of quitting and proffered them medicinal or other forms of aid, it could lead to the salvation of 42,000 lives annually.

There exist ample opportunities for primary care physicians to treat tobacco use and nicotine addiction within their professional sphere. The following activities could aid physicians in harnessing such opportunities 16,21:

Advise all patients regarding the harmful effects associated with the use of nicotine and tobacco products.

Conducting advanced clinical education sessions for all members of the care team, with a focus on efficacious treatment modalities and strategies to overcome obstacles.

Implement or enhance in-office risk-mitigation initiatives and tactics, including those aimed at vulnerable segments of the population.

Establish communication with the medical services team to deliver tobacco cessation counseling and clinical interventions.

Provide a clearly delineated protocol for healthcare providers and practitioners to assess patients' willingness to discontinue medication, encourage cessation for individuals who are not currently interested, facilitate appropriate prescribing and use of discontinuation medications, and offer follow-up care.

Integrate a systematic approach to provide patients with enhanced information and assistance in cessation endeavors, utilizing appropriate members of the healthcare team other than physicians, whenever feasible.

Enumerate the utilization of tobacco as a causal factor of demise when deemed appropriate.

Employ the tobacco consumption status as a pivotal indicator.

Create a comprehensive chart in the patient's medical file that outlines all previous discussions pertaining to smoking cessation and past attempts to quit, as an aid for the attending clinician.

The American Academy of Family Physicians recommends that its members employ a range of counseling techniques to address tobacco use and nicotine addiction, such as motivational interviewing, brief interventions, and group therapy sessions. It is imperative for individuals to recognize and adequately tackle barriers that impede the efficacy of mediation and treatment. Obstacles are present both at the individual level involving patients and doctors, and also at a foundational level.

Boundaries at the level of the patient and the doctor comprises:

Lack of motivation to cease.

Noncompliance with medication and therapeutic sessions.

The employment of treatments that lack a basis in evidence.

Constrained duration of patient interaction.

Primary level delimitations comprise:

An occurrence of contradictory development aimed at ensuring patients adhere to final designs and appropriate references was experienced.

Inadequate remittance and periodic payments for the purpose of final dispensation and interventions.

Ambivalent growth strategy to prompt clients towards utilizing amenities.

What Is Nrt

Nicotine Replacement Therapy (NRT) is a therapeutic approach for smoking cessation that entails the substitution of nicotine inhalation by means of various substitutes, including patches, gum, or lozenges, as well as injections or inhalers.

The evidence substantiating its effectiveness for individuals who smoke at any degree is evident. Nonetheless, it remains uncertain whether comparable benefits can be observed in individuals who smoke at a low frequency, that is, less than ten cigarettes per day. However, the evidence suggests that it is effective for people who smoke heavily.

Who can use it?

It is a beneficial tool for individuals seeking to cease smoking and for those who smoke in excess of ten cigarettes per day.

Who should not use it?

If you possess a medical ailment which renders the utilization of these medicines inadvisable. It is presently not advised to use NRT in children or adolescents.

How does it work?

Nicotine Replacement Therapy (NRT) replenishes the nicotine in your brain that is typically absorbed by inhaling cigarette smoke, through the administration of nicotine patches, gums, or lozenges. It is not addictive.

When and how much?

For optimum efficacy, it is recommended to combine the use of NRT with a comprehensive behavior modification program featuring diverse modalities of smoking cessation, such as the application of patches and therapy. The efficacy of NRT may be diminished for individuals who utilize smoking cessation patches for a consecutive period of five or more days.

Many individuals can curtail or discontinue smoking entirely within a matter of weeks without resorting to NRT; however, it is imperative to bear in mind that the cessation rate for those individuals who utilize NRT is comparatively higher. The majority of cessation efforts are typically short-lived, with individuals tending to abandon their endeavor within a short span of a few days.

How is it provided?

The aforementioned nicotine cessation aids, namely patches, gum, and lozenges, may be obtained through a prescription. However, it is not mandatory to schedule an appointment with your physician to acquire them.

Nicotine replacement therapy may be dispensed by a licensed physician or authorized pharmacy through a prescribed regimen, or alternatively, be obtained over-the-counter as a means of self-administration.

Drug stores and community pharmacies also offer medications such as patches and gum.

Certain regions of Australia provide their citizens with access to nicotine replacement therapy (NRT) via self-guided initiatives, such as the Quitline program.

The Quitline program, offered by the Australian Government, offers telephone-based counseling as well as complimentary patches, gum, and lozenges to aid individuals who are motivated to quit smoking. The Quitline can provide the nicotine replacement medicines needed to help you stop smoking and, if you need more help, can connect you to free online resources and local resources such as Quit Bites (Australia) for those who live in rural and regional areas.

Is it necessary to schedule an appointment with my physician?

In the event of being prescribed NRT, it is recommended to engage in a discussion with a medical professional, whereas over-the-counter patches, gum, and lozenges are procurable without the aforementioned prescription. Nevertheless, the acquisition of NRT from numerous pharmacies shall require a physician's prescription.

One could employ NRT concurrently with alternative smoking cessation therapies such as patches, gum, or self-directed programs.

May I inquire as to the recommended duration of use?

Nicotine Replacement Therapy (NRT) aids individuals who smoke in their smoking cessation journey; however, the process of quitting may require a significant duration. The advantages derived from the application of NRT become apparent in a fortnight of smoking cessation, however, complete benefits do not materialize until a minimum of three months have elapsed. The more prolonged the abstinence from smoking, the greater the likelihood of experiencing optimal health outcomes for individuals.

Using NRT

Nicotine replacement therapy (NRT) has demonstrated efficacy in aiding individuals who engage in smoking cessation. Optimal outcomes are typically achieved when employed therapeutically in conjunction with complementary smoking cessation modalities.

According to research, the efficacy of NRT appears to be greater among individuals who smoke a minimum of ten cigarettes per day. However, the available evidence is inconclusive regarding the effectiveness of NRT among those who smoke less than ten cigarettes per day. It is a widely recognized fact that NRT is not a efficacious therapeutic alternative for individuals who engage in smoking less than ten cigarettes per day. This is primarily due to the fact that your chances of attaining a complete cessation of the habit are relatively low if you rely solely on unaided efforts.

It must be borne in mind that cessation of the activity or habit in question shall be a challenging endeavor. Individuals who cease smoking through the utilization of NRT are recommended to undertake multiple subsequent cessation endeavors to enhance the likelihood of sustaining abstinence from smoking over an extended period.

People who use NRT before trying to quit will need to find a different quit approach (called a 'dual therapy'), as people using NRT will need to manage cravings and maintain their abstinence from smoking. It is achievable to alter one's smoking habits utilizing patches, gum, or lozenges, and it is always viable to terminate smoking at any opportune moment.

What is dual therapy?

The dual therapy approach entails employing a combination of smoking cessation aids such as patches, gum, and a Quitline program, alongside the standard NRT and cessation-only methods. Dual therapy may encompass the implementation of multiple therapeutic techniques, such as the combination of patches and gum, or patches and quitline support.

Is it safe?

There is no enduring detrimental effect associated with the utilization of NRT. It is not addictive. The administration of NRT may be considered in cases where alternative interventions have proven ineffective.

It is imperative to adhere to the guidance provided by your physician or pharmacist, as is the case with all pharmaceuticals.

Withdrawal Symptoms

Individuals attempting to cease smoking cigarettes frequently encounter withdrawal reactions, which can impede their cessation progress. A few of the frequently encountered manifestations of withdrawal ensue, viz. hankerings for cigarettes, irritability, anxiety, cognitive impediments, and augmented appetite.

The desire to smoke tobacco products is a prevalent manifestation of withdrawal. The intensity of these yearnings can be quite overpowering, persisting for a span ranging from a few minutes to several hours. The intensity of tobacco cravings typically reaches its zenith during the initial week of smoking cessation, gradually tapering off thereafter.

Agitation represents a prevalent manifestation of withdrawal. Individuals who engage in smoking behavior may exhibit heightened levels of anger, frustration, and difficulty regulating their emotions. The tendency to become irritable typically abates within a few weeks subsequent to smoker cessation; however, in certain individuals, this phenomenon may persist for several months or even years post-withdrawal.

Anxiety is a frequently encountered experience among individuals who are smokers attempting to cease the habit. It is possible that you may experience a sense of unease or apprehension towards certain things that typically do not affect you, leading to difficulty in obtaining restful sleep. Typically, apprehension reaches its pinnacle in the initial fourteen days subsequent to cessation of smoking, albeit it may endure over an extended period in certain individuals. An additional manifestation commonly observed during smoking cessation is decreased capacity to focus. Individuals may experience a longer than anticipated duration in concentrating on assignments and recalling information.

This symptom is typically of a temporary nature, lasting for a few weeks; however, in some individuals, it may persist over a prolonged period. Heightened craving for food is a frequently documented occurrence among individuals undergoing smoking cessation. Numerous individuals experience an abrupt inclination to consume, particularly indulgent foods."

Nicotine addiction up close

It is crucial for you to acknowledge your nicotine addiction. Prior to attempting to overcome addiction, it is imperative to first achieve acceptance of the situation at hand. Smoking is not pursued for the purpose of pleasure, and its inherent nature does not lend itself to being an enjoyable experience.

I have encountered numerous individuals who despite having indulged in smoking for a prolonged duration, exhibit an unwillingness to acknowledge their addiction. They derive pleasure from such conduct; smoking is a deliberate choice on their part. They purportedly assert their capability to discontinue at any moment. That is until they make an attempt. I have encountered that scenario before and have already experienced it.

Your body has developed a physical dependence on nicotine, to the point where its normal functioning now requires its presence in order for you to feel well. There is nominal distinction between this addiction and other forms of dependence, including heroin.

The issue of physical addiction does not typically pose a challenge for individuals seeking to abstain from smoking. The absence of said symptom manifests within a few weeks of abstaining, thereby denoting a rapid cessation of said symptom. Certain individuals may encounter minor physical withdrawal symptoms; however, managing such symptoms is not overly arduous. The aforementioned symptoms encompass a spectrum, spanning from mild cephalalgias to hyperhidrosis and paresthesias in both the distal upper and lower extremities. The neurobiological system gradually adjusts to a lifestyle habituated to an absence of nicotine. Hence, abstaining from smoking should be a comparatively effortless endeavor. Well, it is not.

The cessation of physical dependence usually occurs within a few weeks, however, in order to ensure sustained progress, it is imperative to address and eliminate psychological dependence as well. It is necessary for you to amend your customary practices and your perspective pertaining to tobacco consumption. Could you kindly elaborate on the precise connotation of my statement? Diverse individuals have differing preferences and requirements. Regrettably, a definitive response to that inquiry is not possible due to the absence of a singularly accurate solution. As evident from the outset of the book, diverse rationales underlie the act of smoking. Certain individuals are of the opinion that smoking assists them in problem-solving and during times of stress, while others maintain that it has a calming effect on them, among other perceptions.

As long as one retains the belief that smoking constitutes a source of benefit or gratification, relinquishing this habit would appear to lack a rationale. If you choose to do so, you would face difficulties in maintaining your non-smoking status. The advent of the initial challenging circumstance is likely to trigger your relapse into smoking. The trigger could be anything - bad day at work, fight with the family or friend, etc. Due to the tremendous addictive properties of nicotine, the consumption of a single cigarette is sufficient to reset one's progress to day one, necessitating the contending of the physical addiction once again.

Prioritize mental clarity before attempting to cease smoking. Do not make excuses. It is imperative to understand that cigarettes do not provide any beneficial aspects for an individual's health and wellbeing.

Addiction cycle

The cerebral mechanism involved in smoking may not appear perceptible, however, researchers are cognizant of its precise functioning. Presently, we have comprehended how physiological reliance operates in conjunction with psychological components. Your engagement in smoking results in an elevation of nicotine levels in your brain. The immediate reduction in nicotine levels initiates a subsequent desire to smoke after a brief interval, typically lasting for an hour or two. Your demeanor displays signs of agitation and irritability. Upon smoking a cigarette, one experiences a sense of immediate well-being. At a subliminal level, the brain forms an association between the sensation of relaxation and smoking. Upon observing a pack of cigarettes, one tend to associate it with the notion of gratification. If you were not afflicted by nicotine dependence, you would observe toxicity. You are currently undergoing a conditioning process that may lead to addiction. Smoking consistently induces relaxation. Subsequently, following a period of time, tension resurfaces and there is a compulsion to smoke, resulting in relaxation. The process of alternating nicotine concentration levels is a perpetual cycle.

Inquire with individuals who abstain from smoking on their perspective regarding tobacco consumption. From their perspective, a pack of cigarettes is not considered to have a favorable connotation. From the smoker's perspective, it is so. I am cognizant of my emotions at the precise moment of my visual encounter with a packet of cigarettes resting on the surface of the table. Like seeing a chocolate. Delicious little things. Since having overcome my nicotine addiction, I now perceive the act of smoking as a harmful and destructive habit. I do not possess any affirmative sentiments or affiliations towards cigarettes at present.

Substance dependency can lead to perceptual hallucinations. It is impossible to cogitate in an unclouded and logical manner concerning the selfsame object that has engendered addiction.

It seems that you may not be aware that the act of smoking potentially serves to fulfill a particular chemical craving within your brain for nicotine. Consider approaching the matter from this perspective. Dependency is a neurological process that manifests within the depths of the brain, while the act of smoking is often observed in open spaces. It would be prudent to engage in a process of rationalization regarding your actions. One must possess the ability to articulate to others the reasons behind smoking and the consequential harm it causes to oneself. In order to achieve this, the mind becomes convinced of the supposed benefits of smoking, falsely believing in their positive effects on the body.

Although it may appear peculiar, it is plausible that your cognitive processes are deceiving you. Perchance, you may not have been cognizant of it. If you were to cease smoking promptly, you would abstain from indulging in the pleasurable substance known as nicotine and prioritize the well-being of your body and mind. Your cognitive faculties exhibit a marked affinity towards this particular substance. In order to maintain your engagement, they must generate a variety of justifications. Carrying cigarettes in your apparel instills a sense of companionship as if having a reliable confidante by your side continuously. "May I inquire whether you hold a similar perspective with regards to those diminutive objects commonly referred to as 'cigarettes', or tobacco?". This is an addictive tendency, my acquaintance.

Upon attaining a comprehensive understanding of the nature of addiction, relinquishing it becomes a substantially smoother process. One may gradually gain an understanding of nicotine's true nature and the effects it has on one's being. Some individuals exhibit a hostile response towards it. Indignant towards cigarettes, for enabling them to exert dominance over one's existence for a prolonged period. The state of being addicted does not confer freedom; rather, it entails being in servitude to the substance in question, regardless of its nature.

You appear to have an inner voice that persistently prompts you to ignite a cigarette. Consistently providing assurances of a notable and desirable encounter and imparting positive sentiments regarding the experience. You are not able to perceive this auditory sensation, naturally. It conceals itself within the depths of one's emotions. It seems that you are experiencing a compulsion to smoke. Consuming a single cigarette can result in a perceived sense of improvement in one's physiological and psychological state. For the ensuing hour or thereabouts. Then the countdown begins. As the level of nicotine depletion commences, the subsequent events can be inferred... The relentless repetition of nicotine addiction is a persistent occurrence, manifesting incessantly over extended stretches of time.

The most admirable aspect of it is that you are under the impression that you are engaging in it for the sake of enjoyment. It appears that you indulge in smoking on an ad hoc basis. It appears that you hold the belief that you are able to exert influence over said actions. Do you really? Would it be possible for you to abstain from smoking for a brief period of a few days without experiencing any anxious feelings? Would it be feasible for you to abstain from smoking for a day or more, without experiencing any intrusive thoughts about tobacco? You cannot. You are an addict. Acceptance, remember?

May I inquire if you continue to deceive yourself with fabricated narratives? If that is indeed the case, then it is apparent that your cognitive capabilities exceed your current estimation. You will need to exert greater effort to outwit them. Overcome addictive behaviors and regain a sense of liberation in your life. At present, you appear to lack autonomy in your life. I apologize for any bluntness, however, the situation stands as it is. The expeditious relinquishment of self-deception, recognition of reality and subsequent initiation of remedial measures can hasten one's pathway towards recuperation. It is recommended that you assert ownership of your life once more.

What is the reason behind the heightened clarity of perception among individuals who do not engage in smoking with regards to the subject matter of smoking? I regret to inform that I am no longer able to endure confined spaces in the presence of smoking individuals. I find it repulsive. How come? I had the opportunity to derive pleasure from the same experience. My cognitive faculties have led me to perceive it in that manner. Having successfully overcome nicotine addiction, I am now able to perceive the smell of cigarette smoke in its true essence, which is evidently unpleasant. You too shall attain the desired outcome, however, it is imperative for you to eliminate the addictive habit beforehand.

When individuals cease smoking, they may pose an inconvenience to fellow smokers. Perchance, you have had a personal encounter with it. You have encountered an individual who has recently quit smoking and has gained considerable knowledge on the detriments of smoking, considering it a reprehensible habit. Ex-smokers become preachers...

Frequently, individuals communicate to me that I ought to temper my behavior, as they perceive it to be conceited, despite my lengthy two decades of smoking, and my zealous efforts to encourage cessation in others. What prompted your present perception towards smoking as being repulsive? It appears that you have a desire to partake in smoking. Would you be willing to acknowledge this? I must express my reluctance towards smoking, as it is not my desire to engage in such an activity. In addition, I firmly believe that upon adopting a non-smoking lifestyle, you too will share in this sentiment. Only upon attaining a comprehensive grasp of the circumstances shall you fully comprehend the state of denial under which you presently dwell.

Engaging in an activity solely for the purpose of satisfying an addiction cannot truly be considered a source of pleasure, can it? Think of sweets. Despite any attempts to reduce our consumption, these delectable treats will remain inherently enticing and appealing. We must proactively manage our desire for sugary foods. Abstaining from consuming sweets for a prolonged period of time notwithstanding, the mere sight of a chocolate cake evokes a pleasurable sensation. It behooves you to exercise self-restraint and deliberate thought in consuming it, lest you partake of it in a single, unbridled moment. You have cravings. Cigarette consumption and smoking do not align with such a notion. Upon cessation of cigarette smoking, it is probable that the aforementioned habit will eventually become repulsive to the individual concerned. Perhaps not in the initial phase, but it is highly likely to occur subsequent to a few months. After successfully overcoming the addictive habit, one's sentimentally charged perception of smoking dissipates. That factor alone will serve as a safeguard against relapse and consequently, prove to be a positive development.

How To Quit Smoking

1. Find Your Reason

In order to attain the state of motivation, it is essential to have a convincing and individualized cause to cease the current undertaking. It may be necessary to take measures to protect one's family from the harmful effects of secondhand smoking. Alternatively, mitigate the chances of developing lung cancer, heart disease or other associated complications. Or in order to exhibit a more youthful appearance and vigor. Select a justification that possesses significant strength capable of surpassing the urge to ignite a cigarette.

2. Engage in Adequate Preparation Prior to Initiating Cold Turkey Approach

There is a greater depth to the matter than simply discarding your cigarettes. Smoking is an addiction. Nicotine is known to cause addictive tendencies in the brain. Devoid of it, you will undergo withdrawal symptoms. Secure the necessary backing beforehand. It is recommended that you consult with your healthcare professional regarding the various methods that could aid you in quitting smoking including but not limited to cessation programs, therapy, medication, and hypnotherapy. You shall be adequately prepared for the day you opt to relinquish your position.

3. Consider Nicotine Replacement Therapy

Ceasing smoking may induce nicotine withdrawal symptoms, such as headaches, mood disturbances, and reduced vitality. It can be tremendously challenging to resist the temptation to indulge in a single puff. Nicotine replacement therapy has the potential to diminish such impulses. Research indicates that the utilization of nicotine gum, lozenges, and patches can enhance the probability of achieving success in smoking cessation endeavors when employed in conjunction with a quit-smoking program.

4. Learn About Prescription Pills

Pharmaceutical interventions have the potential to mitigate urges and diminish the pleasurable effects of smoking, in the event that an individual chooses to partake in cigarette consumption. Alternative medications facilitate an alleviation of withdrawal symptoms including melancholy and cognitive impairment.

5. Rely on the support of your cherished ones.

Kindly inform your acquaintances, kith and kin, and other individuals within your network that you are endeavoring to cease the habit. They possess the potential to serve as a source of inspiration to persist and resist the urge to illuminate, especially in moments of temptation. You may also avail the opportunity to become a part of a support group or partake in a conversation with a professional counselor. Behavioral therapy is a form of treatment that assists individuals in identifying and adhering to strategies for smoking cessation. Even a limited number of sessions may yield positive results.

6. Give Yourself a Break

One of the factors contributing to smoking behavior is that the chemical compound nicotine is known to have a calming effect on individuals. Upon cessation of your current practices, it will be necessary to adopt alternative means of decompression. There are several alternatives. One may engage in physical activity to alleviate stress, enjoy music that they prefer, maintain social connections, receive a professional massage, or allocate time for a hobby or personal interest. Make an effort to steer clear of taxing situations in the initial stages following the cessation of smoking.

7. It is recommended to refrain from consuming alcoholic beverages and avoiding other precipitating factors.

Consuming alcoholic beverages poses a greater challenge in maintaining one's commitment to abstain from tobacco use. Endeavor to limit alcohol consumption during the initial phase of abstinence. Similarly, if it is your usual practice to smoke cigarettes while having coffee, consider switching to tea for a temporary period. If one habitually indulges in smoking post meals, it is advisable to pursue alternative activities such as maintaining oral hygiene, undertaking a leisurely walk, engaging in communication with acquaintances, or resorting to chewing gum as a substitute.

8. Clean House

After extinguishing your final cigarette, it is advisable to dispose of all ashtrays and lighters in your possession. We suggest laundering any attire that emanates a smoky odor, and thoroughly sanitizing your carpets, curtains, and furnishings. Employ air fresheners to eliminate the recognizable aroma. If you have smoked in your vehicle, kindly ensure that you clean it out thoroughly. It would be preferable if one avoids any visual or olfactory stimuli that may evoke memories or associations with smoking.

9. Try and Try Again

Several individuals make repeated efforts before successfully abstaining from smoking. If you choose to ignite a flame, do not lose encouragement. Subsequently, contemplate upon the precipitating factors that may have led to your relapses, encompassing your emotional state and the circumstances of your surroundings. Avail this opportunity to enhance your dedication towards cessation. After having made the decision to attempt abstaining from the habit once more, it is advisable to select a predetermined date for cessation, preferably falling within the next month.

10. Get Moving

Engaging in physical activity facilitates the reduction of nicotine cravings and mitigates specific withdrawal symptoms. When the desire to smoke arises, it is recommended to engage in physical activities such as inline skating or running instead. Engaging in modest activities, including walking your pet or tending to the garden, can prove to be beneficial. The energy expended by your body will aid in mitigating weight gain during the cessation of smoking.

11. Eat Fruits and Veggies

It is not advisable to embark on a weight-loss regimen when abstaining from smoking. Excessive deprivation has the potential to result in adverse consequences. It is recommended to adopt a simplistic approach and prioritize the consumption of nutrient-dense foods such as fruits, vegetables, whole grains, and lean sources of protein. These possess numerous health benefits contributing to the wellness of your entire body.

12. Choose Your Reward

Apart from all the aforementioned health benefits, an added perk of relinquishing smoking is the considerable monetary savings incurred by abstaining from the habit. There exist online calculators that can compute an estimate of an individual's net worth.

Grant yourself a token of appreciation by indulging in a pleasurable expenditure.

13. Always bear in mind that time is in your favor.

Upon cessation, the immediate health benefits become evident and can be savored. After a brief duration of 20 minutes, your heart rate returns to its resting state. Within a 24-hour timeframe, the carbon monoxide level in your blood is restored to its normal state. Within a span of 2 to 3 weeks, it is highly likely that you will witness a decline in the possibility of being susceptible to a heart attack. Over an extended period, there will be a reduction in the probability of developing lung cancer and other malignant diseases.

Day 26

Exercise:

Today, look for the color blue in your surrounding environment. If feasible, allocate the entire day in dedicated pursuit of identifying instances of the color blue within the environs visited. Regardless of the location, be it indoors, outdoors, or during travel, it is recommended to observe the presence of the color blue in the surrounding environment while performing this exercise, whether it be in a bedroom, office, or classroom. If one anticipates the likelihood of forgetting to carry out this task throughout the day, it is recommended to devote a minimum of 20 concentrated minutes to exercise this activity at a convenient interval.

The cultivation of concentrated focus demands consistent practice, given that it is not an innate trait in our fast-paced modern society. Instead of encouraging us to focus and observe, the modern world encourages us to rush and get things done.

In the quest for a suitable color or shape, there is a marked deceleration of our frenetic and cyclical modes of thinking, thereby prompting a realization that existence encompasses more than the turbulent thoughts that we encounter on a collective and quotidian basis. Through the act of seeking out the hue of blue, one may liberate their mind from the hold of pernicious emotions such as anxiety, lust, desire, depression, worry, fear, and the like. Whilst you were indulging in smoking, did you happen to take notice of the striking hues surrounding you? Most likely not.

Smoking serves as a means to divert one's conscience from the current reality. Be mindful to observe the hue of blue in your surroundings today, and seize the opportunity to fully embrace the present moment.

Fifteen minutes of dedicated meditative contemplation and deep breathing. Recite the affirmation: "I am channeling my concentration towards the present moment with utmost clarity and precision."

We kindly request you to share your experience by utilizing the hashtag #30DaysBlue.

Day 27

Exercise:

Engage in a mindful walking practice, allocating a minimum of 10 minutes. Focus on each step. Experience the sensation: focus on the tactile feedback of each stride, including the impact of your footfall, the smooth rotation of your heel, the precise placement of your toes, the subtle flexion of your knees, the concerted effort of your hips to maintain equilibrium, and the synchronized motion of your arms." Don't rush; go slow. Direct your attention towards your respiration as well. Harmonize with your physical being. Be mindful of your sensory perceptions during the course of your stroll. Please concentrate on the task at hand and refrain from engaging in activities such as listening to music or getting distracted.

Throughout history, individuals have consistently utilized ambulation as an organic means of rejuvenating their physical well-being. Engaging in a leisurely stroll and directing one's attention towards the act of walking has a soothing effect on both the psyche and spirit. The more one proceeds on foot, the greater the sensation of relaxation one experiences.

One can seize any opportune instance to take a constitutional and immerse oneself in both the mental and physical surroundings. While embarking on extended walks, one may encounter cognitions that facilitate a deliberate observation thereof. Allow the passing of thoughts and even the arising of emotions, and endeavor to impartially observe and subsequently release them. Directing your attention towards your actions may aid in decluttering your thought process. Engaging in early morning and dusk strolls is particularly advantageous.

A pedestrian stroll lasting for 20 minutes yields more comfort, serenity, tranquility, concentration, and mindfulness than countless hours of smoking cigarettes. Engage in daily ambulation to the fullest extent feasible.

Fifteen-minute duration allotted for practicing mindfulness via tranquil quietude and concentrated respiration. Recite the affirmation: "I am in a state of relaxation." I am experiencing a sense of tranquility."

We kindly request that you disseminate this experience by using the designated hashtag #30DaysWalk.

Day 28

Exercise:

Close your eyes and deliberately perceive your cardiac rhythm for a duration of two to three minutes.

Abstain from enumerating the beats; rather, attune yourself to the cadence. Furthermore, it is advisable not to attempt to alter its tempo. Continue to breathe normally. One can perceive the pulsations of their heart by gently placing two fingers on the side of their neck just beneath the jawbone (carotid pulse), positioning their hand on their chest (bronchial pulse), or by delicately placing two fingers on the inner side of their wrist (radial pulse). Utilize whichever approach provides you with the optimal sensation of your cardiac rhythm. Allow your mind to release any distractions, and concentrate fully on the cadence of your heart pulsating.

It is possible for individuals to remain entirely oblivious throughout their lifetime to the engineering marvel that resides within their chest. Think about it. From the moment of your inception in the uterus, your cardiac muscle initiated its rhythmic contractions, which have remained uninterrupted to this day, and will persist until the termination of your earthly existence. It is an exceptional mechanism that continues to operate until the moment of our ultimate demise. The cardiac muscles decelerate for the purpose of relaxation, yet they persistently perform their duties without cessation. Explore and acquaint yourself with the splendor of your heartfelt emotions and harmonize yourself with its inherent cadence.

Analogous to the practice of mindful attention to one's breath, the act of perceiving the pulsations of one's heart while meditating can facilitate the attainment of a state of heightened present moment consciousness. Exercise caution with regards to your cardiac health, acquaint yourself with its pulse, take adequate measures to care for it, express gratitude for its stamina and power, and permit it to pulsate. When experiencing stress, it is advised to refrain from smoking. Instead, focus on your breath and heartbeat as a means of calming yourself. Why persist in exposing your remarkable heart to harm by consuming tobacco, a substance known to be toxic? Ensure cardiac health by maintaining a healthy heart rate.

Fifteen minutes dedicated to maintaining silence and engaging in mindful respiratory exercises. Recite the affirmation: "My cardiac organ is robust and indispensable for sustaining my existence."

I kindly request that you share this particular experience through the use of the hashtag #30DaysHeart.

Formulating A Strategic Roadmap Employing The Four-Step Pilt Methodology.

The process of Pre-quit Implementation Intentions (PILT) is an efficacious and uncomplicated approach that affords individuals the capacity to strategically plan prior to embarking on a smoking cessation pursuit. By proactively completing these steps beforehand, the probability of accomplishing your objective significantly increases.

Initial step: Identify a definite date upon which you intend to halt the activity in question.

Proceed to Stage 2: Ascertain and anticipate impediments, and proactively strategize to overcome them.

Proceed with the third step by acquainting your physician,

acquaintances, and kin about the matter at hand.

Step 4: Discard all tobacco-related articles.

Allow us to briefly analyze each step at this juncture.

Initial step: Identify a precise date on which you intend to terminate.

The preliminary action is to identify a precise date. When selecting a date, it is advisable to opt for one that is proximate. It is advisable to refrain from setting a notice period of one month for resignation. Selecting an excessively distant goal may result in a considerable decrease in your motivational drive, thereby causing you to lose focus on the underlying factors that led you to initiate your abstinence pursuit. An optimal time period for ceasing smoking is ideally within a span of one to two weeks. By adopting this approach, you shall be adequately equipped with ample time to make all the necessary arrangements. Choose a day on which you are confident that you can manage stress and resist the urge to smoke. Avoid selecting a day preceded by potential stressors such as an imminent big exam or a weekend when your mother in law will be visiting. Upon finalizing your preferred date, kindly record it on your personal calendar for future reference. Ensure that the calendar is positioned in a prominent location that is easily accessible and visible on a daily basis. In the event of not maintaining a personal calendar, it is advised to procure a digital template of the relevant month's calendar from a reliable online source, obtain a hard copy through printing, and exhibit it in a visible location.

Secondly, it is imperative to recognize potential hindrances and strategize proactively in order to address them.

Foreseeing and acknowledging the probable hindrances which might arise during this period, and strategically devising coping strategies, will be imperative for you. Anticipate experiencing symptoms of withdrawal as they may arise. As aforementioned, the addictive substance in tobacco is not the smoke or the tobacco per se, but the nicotine present therein. Ceasing or decreasing the level of nicotine intake that one is habituated to, necessitates the body to undergo a process of adaptation. The aforementioned condition carries the potential to induce disagreeable symptoms, including but not limited to uneasiness, fidgeting, vexation, exhaustion, and various other sources of physical discomfort. Please be aware that the path to relinquishment will be challenging, requiring you to exhibit unwavering fortitude throughout the journey. There exist pharmacological interventions that can be employed during this timeframe for the purpose of managing any withdrawal-related symptoms you might encounter. Several of them are accessible as non-prescription medications. Prioritize the acquisition of knowledge about them by conducting a thorough study and subsequently consulting with your healthcare professional. If you are of the opinion that they will serve your requirements, it is advisable to possess them prior to endeavoring to withdraw. It is reassuring to note that the most severe withdrawal symptoms subside within a matter of days upon quitting. Adopting a more moderate approach will ensure that the severity of your symptoms is minimized. During moments of fragility or susceptibility, individuals may elect to reach out to their loved ones or seek support from reputable crisis lines for assistance. One of the available hotlines for assistance can be reached by dialing the toll-free number 1-800-QUIT-NOW. An array of mobile applications also exist that can assist you in cessation of the habit.

This list serves the purpose of promoting proactive thinking regarding future events and cultivating a sense of foresight in anticipation of potential challenges, all the while equipping you with strategies to overcome any obstacles that may arise along the way. If proactive measures are not taken in advance, the ability to devise a practical solution in the moment may be impeded due to lack of determination. Hence, it is advisable to have a pre-conceived solution in place, documented thoroughly and readily accessible to you. You are expected to assimilate information and adhere to regulations, considering the possibility that your mental fortitude may not withstand challenges.

Proceed to the third step by informing your physician, acquaintances, and relatives.

If individuals in your social circle predominantly refrain from smoking, they are liable to provide you with greater impetus to discontinue the habit. In every instance, the process of resigning shall prove to be less strenuous provided that you acquire their backing. State clearly the specific ways in which they can render assistance and support, while conveying that their presence is most valuable at present. Given the circumstances, it is evident that you do, in fact. At times, seeking assistance may seem arduous, yet in this particular situation, you shall find solace in having done so. Additionally, it is imperative that you maintain ongoing communication with your healthcare provider. Your medical practitioner can conduct a thorough assessment of your physical well-being and provide you with advice pertaining to maintaining your focus towards your objective. Furthermore, should abstinence prove challenging, the healthcare provider may propose the adoption of a nicotine replacement therapy regimen. This entails the utilization of nicotine-based products, including patches and sprays, to facilitate one's cessation of smoking and break their addiction to the nicotine-induced euphoria. Further elaboration on this topic shall be provided in subsequent sections of this publication.

Proceed with Step 4 by disposing of all items that are associated with smoking.

Ultimately, it is imperative that you eradicate all cigarettes from your dwelling, as well as any paraphernalia which may serve as a reminder, including but not limited to ash receptacles, lighters, and matches. Please ensure that you dispose of any cigarette residues in your vehicle, including emptying the ashtray and eliminating any cigarette butts that may have been left inside. If there exist any areas, such as your attic or garage, that emanate cigarette smoke, it is imperative that measures be taken to alleviate such odor. Dispose of each and every cigarette. It is advisable to refrain from retaining a pack for hypothetical situations. In the event of an unintended lapse, it is recommended that one is obliged to exert themselves by venturing to the retail establishment to acquire a packet of cigarettes. Maintaining a stash of cigarettes at home as a precautionary measure renders an individual susceptible to yielding to temptation.

Section two: Colleague Counselor

Through the assistance and support of one's companions...

23. Find a quit-buddy.

Are you acquainted with the adage that states, "Collaboration between two individuals yields superior outcomes than working alone... Should they stumble, one individual shall assist their companion in rising.

After arriving at a resolution to discontinue, communicate with your acquaintances and relatives, as your actions may serve as an impetus for them to follow suit. It is commendable when both partners make a collaborative decision to cease together.

24. Be accountable to someone.

In case you lack a cessation companion, it is advisable to enlist the support of a dependable friend or relative as your designated accountability partner. This individual serves as the primary point of contact for those seeking a listening ear, a sounding board, emotional support, or jubilation. This is the very individual upon whom you may rely upon to lend succor in moments of dejection while you are attempting to cease a habit; the individual who possesses the requisite expertise to invigorate and embolden you, even if it implies resorting to stern measures.

25. Rely on the support and assistance of your close family and friends.

Individuals in close proximity to your personal sphere possess the capacity to aid you in overcoming this formidable circumstance.

Establish a professional network of individuals whom you may rely on for support in any circumstance.

Please redirect your attention to the words in italics as mentioned previously: net and fall.

Envision your loved ones as a support network, providing a safeguard against feelings of total solitude.

26. Talk.

The human species possesses remarkable qualities and characteristics. (I know there are exceptions to this rule, but bear with me for the sake of this illustration). During the initial phases of smoking cessation, individuals may find themselves in various settings wherein they may encounter sudden nicotine cravings or withdrawals.

An effective approach to address the issue would be to initiate a conversation with individuals in your immediate surroundings. One may find themselves standing in line at a Starbucks establishment, where the aroma of coffee can evoke a desire for the beverage. Alternatively, one may find themselves waiting at a bus stop where they are unsure of how to occupy their hands. Initially, it may be challenging to predict the timing or location of the impulses.

Endeavor to engage in conversation with individuals in your immediate vicinity and disclose to them the duration of time that has elapsed since you last consumed a cigarette. It is highly likely that you shall have the delightful experience of crossing paths with individuals who have adeptly ceased smoking and are capable of providing substantial inspiration. Even individuals who are entirely unknown to us have the capacity to provide verbal reinforcement during moments of necessity.

27. Listen.

Permit individuals who have already ceased their participation to recount their narratives to you. Not only will you offer others the chance to validate their success, but you will also derive inspiration from their achievements.

In a comparable vein, lend an ear to the tales of individuals who have endeavored to cease smoking but were unsuccessful in their aspirations. It is possible that their journey may provide you with some valuable insights.

28. Pilot yourself.

Whilst it may prove advantageous to lend an ear to the counsel and anecdotes proffered by others, it behooves one to bear in mind that the ultimate responsibility of prevailing in this struggle rests solely upon oneself. Despite the successes or failures of those who preceded you, their experiences are not indicative of your own unique circumstances and abilities. Given the divergent nature of their body chemistry from yours, it follows that the ensuing reactions of your respective bodies are apt to vary.

Ensure that you devise your own game plan and strategy to augment your chances of success, and refrain from solely depending on another individual's 'Top 10 Tips'.

29. Support groups.

Support groups are available for individuals who are seeking to abstain from smoking. It proves beneficial to associate with individuals who possess a comprehensive understanding of the circumstances you are experiencing. In case anonymity is preferred, online support groups also exist as a potential option.

30. Stop smoking clinics.

Enroll yourself in a specialized clinic that provides assistance to individuals striving to overcome their addiction to nicotine. Furthermore, in addition to receiving responsive support, you will be bestowed with the supplementary advantage of professional medical guidance pertaining to alternative methods that may aid in reducing your body's reliance on nicotine.

31. Social networking.

Initiate a written record in the form of a blog that documents your journey towards achieving a nicotine-free state. Your blog has the potential to inspire or encourage individuals.

Calculation of one's days on social media platforms such as Facebook or Twitter is not a productive use of time. Commence by notifying your acquaintances and adherents about your resolution to discontinue smoking; subsequently, conclude each accomplished day by enumerating the number of days you have abstained from smoking.

If your acquaintances on the virtual platform come across the numeric value of '15' on your status or post update, it shall convey a clear message to them and their appreciative gestures in the form of 'likes' would further encourage you.

Kindly share an image on Instagram capturing the disposing of your cigarettes.

Kindly endeavor to share images capturing the progressive filling of your receptacle dedicated to the storage of monetary funds, whilst also including tasteful depictions of instances where you partake in self-gratification.

32. The red card.

Using a pair of scissors, fashion the red cardboard into square-shaped pieces with dimensions corresponding to those of a standard business card.

Distribute one of these squares among your family and acquaintances as you communicate your resolution to abstain from smoking.

Kindly request that they retain possession of it, within the confines of their wallet or purse.

In a possible scenario, if you encounter an unfavorable situation that impacts your mood negatively, you may display signs of annoyance, impatience, or even aggression.

During such occasions, individuals in possession of a red card reserve the right to display it.

This is a cheerful and pre-planned mode of communication that is utilized by your near and dear ones to inform you of any instances where you may not be exhibiting pleasant behavior.

Resist behaving akin to a football player by engaging in a dispute with the referee. Your closest companions and loved ones are present to support you, however, it is imperative to desist from exhibiting undesirable conduct. (Smile!)

Section 3: Diet and Drinks

33. Your appetite.

When ceasing the habit of smoking, it is likely that one's appetite shall witness an increase.

Why? Nicotine proves to be an efficacious appetite suppressant due to its chemical properties.

The extent of weight gain is contingent upon the individual's reaction to the increase in appetite. Opting for nutritious snacks can assist in controlling weight retention.

Gaining weight subsequent to smoking cessation is generally negligible, as this withdrawal manifestation is transitory and lasts only for a few weeks, after which, your body begins to recalibrate towards better wellness practices.

34. Chew gum.

To date, there has been no scientific exposition attesting to the efficacy of chewing gum. To articulate it in a succinct manner, indulging in the act of chewing gum post smoking cessation is beneficial as it provides oral stimulation, consequently aiding in the process.

35. Eat fruit and vegetables.

The use of nicotine has resulted in detrimental effects on your physical well-being. To facilitate the elimination of harmful toxins and provide your body with the chance to recuperate, consume fresh produce such as fruits and vegetables. This will furnish your physique with indispensable vitamins, minerals, antioxidants, and phytochemicals to reinstate a salubrious equilibrium.

36. Don't diet.

Seriously. It would be advisable not to attempt weight reduction and smoking cessation simultaneously.

If you attempt to abruptly deprive yourself of a substantial amount, it may result in complete abandonment of your goal.

Amid these trying circumstances, it is advised that you carefully consider the preceding points on the effects of heightened appetite and the benefits of incorporating fruits and vegetables into your diet, while still allowing yourself to consume foods of your choosing.

Certain dietary choices may influence an individual's predisposition to cigarette cravings, while others may attenuate the desire to smoke. Please refer to points 38 and 39 for further information.

37. Don't skip meals.

Owing to the appetite-suppressing properties of nicotine, it is likely that you might have been able to forego meals during your smoking tenure. It is recommended to maintain a consistent dietary regimen as your system adjusts to the cessation of smoking. It is advisable to consume five small meals each day so as to prevent any fluctuations in blood sugar levels that can potentially worsen the withdrawal symptoms.

38. Food and beverages that exacerbate the desire for nicotine.

As previously stated, you possess unique characteristics and your physiological response may differ from that of other individuals.

This compilation of food and beverages serves as a concise overview of the potential items that individuals have discovered to intensify their urge for nicotine.

Glucose activates the mesolimbic pathway involved in the process of experiencing pleasure in the brain. Consuming food items with high sugar levels may lead to an escalated desire for nicotine.

The consumption of alcoholic beverages may exacerbate the difficulty of quitting.

This phenomenon can be attributed to the common practice of simultaneous ingestion of alcohol and tobacco. Your cerebral cortex has established a cognitive connection that has linked alcohol and tobacco. This necessitates prudence in abstaining from alcohol until such time when your nicotine addiction is completely overcome. Once more, it should be noted that this is subject to the individual circumstances of each individual.

Consumption of coffee may trigger nicotine cravings.

This can be attributed, in part, to the fact that many individuals associate coffee consumption with tobacco use.

Additionally, scientific research suggests that nicotine diminishes the rate at which the body processes caffeine in individuals who smoke, relative to those who do not partake in such activity.

Consequently, upon the elimination of nicotine from your system, your body shall respond in a dissimilar manner to caffeine.

Maintaining alkalinity in your diet for a period can prove beneficial as the presence of acidity can protract the retention of toxins within your system.

Some foods elevate the body's acidity levels, such as grains, sugar, milk and specific dairy products, processed foods, red meat, carbonated beverages, other sugary drinks, and protein-dense foods.

39. Foods and beverages that alleviate nicotine cravings.

Presented herewith is a comprehensive inventory of comestibles and beverages that have been reported by other individuals as efficacious in mitigating their urge for nicotine.

Non-sparkling drinks such as fruit juices, non-effervescent water, or herbal infusions.

Specifically, vegetables such as carrots and celery.

Tomatoes, whether in their uncooked form, as tomato sauce, or in the form of ketchup, are included in this list.

Offering either oranges as a fruit or pure orange juice as a beverage option.

Both oats and oat bran are recommended dietary sources.

Potable liquid substance that is colorless, odorless, tasteless, and transparent, which is found in nature and serves as a critical component for the survival of all living organisms. The consumption of water is highly beneficial as it aids in the elimination of harmful substances from one's body.

Vitamin E and Selenium aid in combating illnesses that are correlated with smoking.

It has been established that quitting smoking and using these products can decrease the incidence of heart attacks and lung cancer among individuals.

40. Herbs that help.

There are specific medicinal plants that have been known to reduce anxiety and stress levels, and they have also been found to potentially alleviate symptoms of withdrawal, decrease cravings, and assist with the process of purifying both the lungs and the body.

We have curated a catalogue of herbs, accompanied by a concise portrayal of their advantages concerning the cessation of smoking.

Calamus, also recognized as Acorus calamus, aids in the elimination of harmful substances from the lungs that may be left behind after smoking.

It comprises attributes that possess the potential to alleviate anxiety, in addition to facilitating heightened energy levels and endurance amid phases of abstention.

The administration of catnip has been shown to decrease anxiety and may facilitate the amelioration of insomnia.

It proves to be advantageous for addressing gastrointestinal disorders and headaches, which are frequently linked with the process of nicotine cessation.

Coltsfoot has expectorant properties that facilitate the process of coughing and aid in the expulsion of mucous. It is recommended to employ this remedy judiciously for facilitating the elimination of deleterious phlegm from your respiratory system.

Horsetail contains minute amounts of nicotine and could potentially mitigate withdrawal symptoms during the initial days of cessation. Prolonged consumption is discouraged.

Hyssop facilitates the alleviation of mucous congestion and aids in purifying the respiratory system.

In addition, it aids in calming the central nervous system, alleviating feelings of anxiousness, and promoting heightened cognitive acuity.

It facilitates the elimination of harmful substances from the digestive tract, urinary bladder, and renal organs, thereby potentially reducing the duration of the period of withdrawal symptoms.

Korean Ginseng can facilitate a more effective adaptation of your body to the emotional strains arising from the cessation of smoking.

It has the potential to enhance both vitality and endurance. Enhancement of focus and reduction of restlessness may potentially ameliorate one's emotional state during the phase of withdrawal.

Licorice can also be spelled as liquorice. In this particular context, our reference is directed towards the botanical root structure and not the confectionery item. Masticating on licorice root sticks may alleviate the oral dependency associated with tobacco consumption.

Lobelia generates comparable effects in the brain as nicotine, but without inducing the same level of harm, and it is devoid of addictive properties.

Furthermore, the substance possesses unique qualities that may aid in the purification of the respiratory system while inhibiting involuntary spasms of coughing.

Passionflower facilitates relaxation and tranquility, while mitigating irritability. As such, it has the potential to mitigate instances of insomnia and anxiety that may arise during the process of withdrawal.

Rhodiola offers a myriad of advantages for individuals endeavoring to quit smoking.

It is possible that it could potentially alleviate withdrawal symptoms.

One possible alternative is: "It exerts a beneficial influence on the human body's ability to cope with both psychological and physiological stressors."

It is plausible that its consumption could result in elevated levels of energy, enhanced muscular power, and greater endurance.

3: It has the potential to mitigate the weight gain that may ensue after smoking cessation since it curtails the cortisol levels in the body that attribute to the accumulation of abdominal fat.

Rhodiola has the potential to enhance overall health and promote cognitive abilities.

St. John's Wort facilitates relaxation, alleviates stress, and potentially fosters a positive outlook.

The respiratory advantages of this product comprise the expulsion of pulmonary secretions and the restoration of the adverse effects induced by tobacco use.

It will facilitate the elimination of harmful substances from your circulatory system.

Valerian is most prominently distinguished due to its capability to induce muscle relaxation and sedation. Optimal administration of the substance is recommended during the late hours of the day, as it facilitates the induction of slumber amidst the occurrence of insomnia caused by the cessation of nicotine consumption.

Please be advised that certain herbs may result in unfavorable side effects, particularly when consumed in conjunction with other herbs, medication, or if you suffer from specific medical conditions. Prior to consuming any herbal supplements, it is highly recommended to consult with a qualified professional and adhere to the designated instructions and recommended dosages with utmost care.

Foundational Principles For Transforming Ingrained Patterns Of Behavior.

The process of altering habits ultimately pertains to the outcome. If you still

If one refrains from smoking, they can lead a satisfying existence.

It is perfectly fine, you are making progress. You've defined your

Vocation and any prospective course of action, or the potential absence thereof.

The task upon which you are currently engaged seems to be

The appropriate choice for your discernment. To elaborate further, in the event that you are

When attempting to overcome addiction, it is advisable to engage in activities that are most comfortable and suitable for your current circumstances. Instead of adopting a rigid approach that outlines the exact requirements for recuperation, conventional wisdom suggests that it would be more advantageous to pursue and discover a methodology that best suits an individual's needs.

Where to start?

When presented with a proposal or strategy for change, it is imperative to approach it with a realistic perspective. It is important to acknowledge that all proposed changes ought to be regarded as a set of recommendations. Considering the effectiveness of a plan, would you speculate that the resultant outcomes are primarily influenced by the recommendations offered by the program, or rather, do you believe that individual actions play a pivotal role?

What level of complexity can be attributed to a plan of change?

The efficacy of a given action is contingent not on the action itself, but on the manner in which it is executed. Take into account the true nature and essence of a plan. We

May I provide an analysis in the following manner:

1. Refraining from or ceasing to engage in a particular activity or behavior.

2. Formulating a concrete strategy for abrupt cessation and devising a comprehensive plan for the phase following the abrupt cessation.

3. Facilitating collaborative assistance and mutual aid in a professional network.

4. Individual growth and advancement prior, subsequent, and throughout the implementation of the plan.

5. Remain flexible and ready to modify your strategy as circumstances evolve.

Truly, where lies the enigma in that? It all sounds

quite simple doesn't it? Undoubtedly, there exist several other constituents to my proposed strategy? Prior to any assertions, it is important to note that attaining the said goal may not necessarily be a straightforward or effortless endeavor.

Repeatedly, individuals exhibit a reluctance to modify their behavior. It is a common occurrence for individuals to experience failures due to the inherent nature of being human. However, the underlying contention of my statement is that the plan, in and of itself, lacks significant enigma. The solutions can be found through implementation. A transformation manifests when the individual who has contended to abstain from nicotine usage from the outset is no longer endeavoring to sustain their abstinence. They attain a sense of serenity within themselves and experience a noticeable enhancement in their performance. There may be two possible outcomes, either they successfully recover or they may potentially experience a relapse. Notwithstanding, the concept of transition holds true.

Transformation is categorized into modifications occurring over brief intervals and those taking place over extended periods. For starters,

We adopt distinctive and tailored measures to remain focused on our objectives. If we do not fundamentally revise our approach and transition towards a lasting transformation, we risk the possibility of failure once more. In order to attain long-term success, it is imperative that we institute changes.

At the initiation of the plan, it is essential for us to achieve specific objectives.

We must adhere to our predetermined goals at designated intervals in order to maintain our integrity until the completion of the task. It is worth noting that individual circumstances may vary, however, the basic tenets remain unchanged. A robust system of support, ample structure, and possible provision of protective measures, such as those offered by a treatment facility, may prove indispensable in safeguarding against relapse and ensuring sustained recovery.

Nonetheless, it is imperative to note that these measures are insufficient in guaranteeing long-term cleanliness and sobriety in the absence of constant vigilance against the perils of regression.

Those individuals who fail to adopt a sustainable, comprehensive lifestyle will inevitably experience a decline in their overall well-being.

Reverting to their previous conduct. The conscious identification of the transition from short-term change to long-term change eludes individuals. It's a process.

t just happens. You possess an innate capacity to retrospectively examine your personal growth journey.

up on stage. May I inquire as to the methodology for determining the appropriate course of action? What steps can we take to facilitate a sustained and enduring transformation? The response to that inquiry pertains to the essence of the primary theory. The solution rests in a triad of primary methodologies:

1) It is imperative to recognize and embrace one's inherent worth and dignity as a human being. Confidence.

Establish connections and cultivate professional relationships with individuals in relevant industries through networking opportunities. Support.

Drive towards comprehensive growth and development. Use everything available.

Especially noteworthy is the pivotal role played by the holistic maturation drive.

Element of your transformation from a tobacco user to a tobacco abstainer. Nevertheless, I am uncertain that one can expressly strategize for such a form of expansion. It is imperative to conquer the notion of prioritizing one's plan over education, career, and other aspects, and to avoid giving in to the stresses of life.

Conventional approaches do not foster an all-encompassing growth, hence, if you prioritize...

By disregarding the aforementioned opportunities, you risk hindering your future prospects for expansion. Regardless, the process of maturation necessitates alteration. We must either embrace progress and evolve through change, or regress and fall behind. My proposal to you is to proactively seek out opportunities for holistic development at the initial stages. Explore avenues for expansion and development beyond the limitations of conventional transformation.

This may involve endeavors such as embarking on a fitness routine or altering one's dietary habits.

Commencing mindfulness practice, engaging in physical exercise, acquiring a skill in an art form, expanding one's knowledge through learning new abilities, cultivating fresh connections with others, and so forth. The moment you surpass the unambiguous objective of your initial transformation endeavors marks the onset of transition. When we are engaged in devising a customized traditional strategy, our approach tends to be focused and limited in scope, wherein all possibilities for development are perceived as uni-dimensional.

Arguably, the notion may have been rendered more coherent owing to the structured and sequential arrangement of the twelve-step model that typically follows a set order.

Even within the realm of holistic living and medicine, the process of maturation can be characterized by broadening horizons and a lack of limitation.

linear. Regardless of the undertaking, it is not uncommon for individuals to experience non-linear growth in the face of change. Individuals may demonstrate divergent rates of progress according to their own set of circumstances and innate capabilities. To begin with, several individuals tend to linger for a certain period, endeavoring to establish equilibrium and overcome the impulses and impulses that arise on a daily basis. Day by day. Following our diligent pursuit of comprehensive development, we may undergo a sudden and rapid transformation. To clarify, it is necessary at times to endure challenging circumstances in order to observe even the slightest progress resulting from our efforts within the plan.

The eventual fruition is observed upon the culmination of all endeavors towards a comprehensive development.

Will gradually exhibit returns commensurate with the ongoing investment. The principal impediment to persistent transformation is a state of complacency. After having abstained from nicotine, we have successfully overcome daily cravings as well as more subtle challenges of transformation including feelings of discontentment, hostility, vexation, and despondency. Instead, the true obstacle in achieving sustainable transformation lies in the continuous pursuit of personal growth and development. Direct your attention towards the aforementioned top three techniques and consistently strive to advance your skills, and the tendency towards satisfaction with the status quo will automatically dissipate. Upon commencing our transformation, there exist certain consequential actions we can undertake in order to embark on a positive trajectory. Herein lie actionable measures that we can undertake.

For example:

Participate in any prescribed treatment sessions or scheduled self-improvement programs. Please make every effort to attend any scheduled meetings.

Contact other individuals undergoing recovery and engage in discussions regarding mutual advancement. Examine the existing body of literature on change or craft a comprehensive and systematic plan delineating each stage.

These are the types of suggestions that are typically recommended to individuals who are inexperienced in this matter. How

come? Why? I hear you ask. Because they work. Simply, because they work. They help. It is best to challenge yourself to mature as you change and develop and develop as a spiritual being.

What does this imply? It implies that rather than forsaking your predicaments

Instead of relentlessly expressing dissatisfaction in every meeting, it is advisable to channel your efforts towards more productive avenues while adapting to the alteration. An approach to attain this objective could entail furnishing assistance and guidance for addiction to individuals. Is it not commonly expressed that instructing a particular subject is the most effective means of acquiring expertise in it?

One may also endeavor to explore fresh avenues for personal and professional development beyond the limitations of...

traditional change. As an illustration, the twelve-step program conventionally centers on the enhancement of spiritual development to the exclusion of other aspects. The aforementioned perspective is limited in its scope, and for complete recuperation, it is essential to address various facets of one's life, encompassing physical, emotional, and social aspects. In order to achieve genuine recovery, it is imperative that one adopts a way of living that aligns with this approach. In a manner that contributes to the facilitation of others' needs.

Step 1

Connect to Your Purpose

It is a general observation that individuals do not end their smoking habits in the absence of a compelling motive.

I would like to express my utmost vulnerability to you regarding my complete journey throughout my duration as a smoker. My initiation into smoking commenced when I was approximately fifteen years old and my final experience with smoking occurred during my early thirties. I am unable to provide a specific date for my departure, which distinguishes me from the majority of individuals who resign. It does not appear to be scheduled or recorded in my calendar. My recollection is limited to the knowledge that the occurrence took place on a particular Sunday in the month of August, approximately three to four years in the past.

Throughout my previous habit of smoking, I experienced intermittent periods of usage and cessation, and it wasn't until I had reached my late twenties that my smoking habit intensified to a significant degree. During that period, one contributing factor to my smoking behavior was the observation that a significant number of attractive young ladies engaged in the activity. Upon my discernment, I realized that frequenting the designated smoking area outside a bar or nightclub facilitated the initiation of conversations, as it served as a common meeting spot for all patrons.

Initially, I would merely carry a lighter in my possession and socialize, however, subsequently, I transformed into an individual consistently possessing a pack of cigarettes. My propensity towards addiction escalated abruptly. Despite my cessation of attending bars and clubs and eliminating the need to build new acquaintanceships, following my matrimonial vows and the commencement of child-rearing, I persisted with the habit of smoking, notwithstanding the nullification of its initial objective.

I adopted smoking as I perceived it to enhance my social image. Throughout my tenure as a smoker, I endeavored to cease this undesirable habit on numerous occasions for various reasons. One of the primary hindrances I encountered during my attempts at smoking cessation was the persistent influence of individuals in my social circle, who would offer me cigarettes and encourage me to postpone my quitting to a later time." Kindly consider having just one, as it would not pose a significant issue."

I did not encounter substantial peer influence, yet it was observable that upon discontinuing smoking, individuals within my social circle who were smokers experienced a degree of isolation. When an individual persists in their negative decision despite your warranted reservations, you risk becoming a reflection of their poor judgment. Moreover, if they succeed in deterring you from resigning, it assuages their sense of culpability.

May I inquire as to the rationale behind your decision?

At a certain juncture, one may assert, 'I refuse to endure this any longer.' I must endeavor to effect a modification until a definitive purpose is identified. The acquisition of such purpose will be crucial in facilitating a cessation of this entrenched behavior.

Despite my efforts to quit smoking out of concern for my uncle's passing and apprehension about potential long-term health complications, I was unable to successfully abstain from the habit. Despite persistent graphic warning labels and pictorial representations of the perils of smoking on every cigarette pack across the globe, individuals continue to indulge in smoking. The long-term cautionary measure has proven to be ineffective.

An area of emphasis in this written work will revolve around facilitating the cultivation of salubrious practices linked to your fundamental motivation, namely, the particular rationale behind your decision to refrain from smoking.

The fundamental motivation behind my actions, upon gazing into my daughter's gaze at that precise moment, was to remain alongside her, to extend my support, and to become an improved paternal figure. That principle became the cornerstone of my beliefs. Despite my sincere attempts to relinquish my habit, motivated by aspirations of providing my spouse with a more comfortable livelihood and sparing her from encountering olfactory distress, my efforts proved futile.

What is the underlying motivation or principle that drives your actions and goals?

It is imperative to discern one's goals in life while determining the underlying cause of the desire to resign. As the amount of daily time at your disposal is limited, it is advisable that you prioritize and concentrate on undertaking the tasks that yield the highest returns. It involves comprehending what holds true significance for you and establishing a regimen that upholds your livelihood.

By thoroughly deliberating on the comprehensive range of advantages, and taking into consideration every facet of your existence, our aim was to facilitate a simplified decision-making process for you by posing this question at the outset. It is advisable to select a fundamental objective with which you strongly identify. There is no requirement for it to match mine precisely. Perhaps, one of the primary determining factors for you is the aversion towards having unclean teeth. Identify the reason that resonates with you the most and firmly adhere to that option.

It would be advisable to opt for a fundamental objective that can be attained in the short-run as well. Short-term objectives possess greater efficacy. When a distant objective is set, our efforts are amplified as we strive to achieve it and mentally depict its attainment. Only a small fraction of individuals have the capacity to establish a comprehensive strategy spanning a decade and a half and remain steadfast in fulfilling it.

When individuals become attached to distant objectives, it may prove to be exceedingly challenging to maintain the required perseverance due to the constant battle against temptations. Initially, this pertains to adhering to a routine that can be readily accomplished at present. During the initial weeks and months subsequent to my smoking cessation, the process of refraining from smoking was a daily endeavor. The conceptual framework of anonymous programs, such as Alcoholics Anonymous and Narcotics Anonymous, is primarily premised on the philosophy of contending with a single day at a time.

Our objective is to concentrate on achieving a victory every single day. Upon achieving a consecutive victory for seven days, one would have completed a week. Upon successfully achieving a consecutive winning streak of thirty days, an entire month shall have been won. The process under development entails setting a goal that is in close proximity, sufficiently stimulating you to emerge victorious in your daily pursuits.

Instances of fundamental reasons that one can employ

There exists a multitude of exemplary instances of fundamental objectives at your disposal. The foremost factor is either the presence of sickness or the apprehension thereof. I endured over twelve varied respiratory conditions and complications, yet they failed to compel me to cease. However, the apprehension of coping with emphysema or the prospect of utilizing a breathing apparatus or an oxygen container could be the focal point of your concern.

Arguably, the most compelling reason for you may be to prioritize one's health. You aspire to increase your pace, revisit your running ability, rejuvenate your youthful vigor, and regain the flexibility and agility to perform physical activities such as jumping jacks and dodgeball. The aspiration to engage in the sports of one's earlier years or partake in long yearned for activities can serve as a driving force and instill a sense of determination.

Another compelling reason could be the familial bond. Perhaps one has faced the loss of a family member, desires to establish meaningful connections with others, or aspires to serve as a positive influence in someone's life.

Fear works well too. If one harbors a fear of the consequences associated with mortality or disease, such apprehension has the potential to serve as a compelling impetus. Apprehension is an incredibly potent sentiment, and you will discover that during episodes of enticement, trepidation triumphs over yearning. This will aid you in surpassing obstacles and persevering towards your objective.

Ultimately, stress could potentially be the root cause of your situation. The act of smoking induces anxiety, which is essentially a variant of lingering or persistent daily trepidation. Continuous contemplation on smoking cessation, coupled with a sense of being trapped in a vicious cycle, could lead to heightened stress levels. In such a scenario, it may be worthwhile to consider the possibility of alleviating this stress and reducing blood pressure through daily focus.

One may consider acquiring a blood pressure apparatus at an approximate cost of $25, which would permit them to assess their blood pressure levels regularly, much like myself. As you refrain from smoking, you may observe a noticeable decline in the measurements displayed on the aforementioned device. Hence, whenever you experience the urge to smoke, kindly insert your limb into the said apparatus and activate it by pressing the button. Subsequently, after a duration of thirty seconds, the enticement dissipates as a sense of contentment emerges from one's accomplishments.

Is it necessary for me to provide a reason or rationale for my actions or decisions?

The Western cultural landscape has undergone a transformation over the past century wherein immediate gratification is increasingly prioritized. Prior to the advancements in credit card technology in the previous century, a substantial number of Americans had accumulated a considerable amount of savings. If one desires to purchase an exceptional Christmas gift for their offspring or loved ones, they may opt for the method of 'layaway', a practice that is scarcely prevalent in contemporary times. Layaway is a service provided by the store wherein a customer selects an item and requests the store to reserve it for subsequent purchase. A partial payment is made in advance over a period of weeks or months, and the item is not delivered until the full payment has been received.

It is the complete antithesis to a credit card. Utilizing a credit card facilitates the procurement of an item with subsequent deferred payment, accompanied by an accrued interest rate which typically exceeds the initially quoted cost. In contemporary times, there is a common perception that layaway is a practice intended solely for individuals of low socioeconomic standing. However, it must be noted that layaway is, in reality, a highly prudent and financially judicious method. Individuals who utilize the layaway system to complete payment for a purchase have exhibited a commendable quality that I deeply admire, as it is rare among our populace. Our societal expectations have become accustomed to immediate satisfaction.

To what extent do individuals publicize their dietary commitments on digital platforms merely to derive immediate sensations of validation? We seek the pleasure without exerting the necessary labor, and thus necessitates the presence of a genuine motivation behind our actions. The satisfaction, positive emotions, and encouragement we may receive from quitting smoking are ephemeral and insufficient to sustain us throughout the entire cessation process.

It is imperative to cultivate an intrinsic drive for motivation as opposed to relying on external recognition as a form of validation.

Previous attempts at smoking cessation have exhibited a recurring cycle of failure. So far, the approach has not yielded the desired results for you. You might have come across the statistical data published by the Centers for Disease Control and Prevention. A significant proportion of individuals among high school smokers have endeavored to abstain from smoking or express a desire to do so, while a substantial proportion of adults, comprising 70% of the population, have made attempts to quit within the previous year. One can be assured that a significant factor contributing towards the unsuccessful outcome of various endeavors was the absence of a fundamental guiding principle.

Furthermore, it is often observed that we tend to engage in the practice of accumulating habits as a pile rather than creating a habit stack which is more efficient. A habit pile refers to the practice of attempting to simultaneously alter numerous aspects of one's behavior or routine. I would like to clarify that I am not without faults and imperfections, and I hope to avoid any misunderstandings regarding my character. I must humbly acknowledge that I do not exhibit impeccable conduct, etiquette, interpersonal associations, or physical presentation. I am an individual who has progressed further up the path in regards to smoking as compared to yourself.

My physique is far from being flawless. Despite my repeated attempts to abstain from smoking, I regrettably relapsed multiple times. Moreover, every time that I succeeded in quitting smoking for a duration, I inevitably succumbed to the infamous phenomenon of weight gain. Following the cessation of my smoking habit, I achieved weight neutrality initially, but eventually lapsed in my vigilance and experienced an increase in body weight. Approximately one year subsequent, as a result of successfully refraining from smoking without experiencing weight gain, I subsequently indulged in the gratification of adding weight as a form of self-reward. I committed an egregious oversight.

But here's the thing. Subsequent to that, I have incorporated additional habits pertaining to physical fitness. I have been consistently experiencing a downward trend in my weight. It is recommended to refrain from attempting to incorporate multiple habits simultaneously. Endeavor not to attempt weight loss and smoking cessation simultaneously. Success can be attained by following a methodical, step-by-step approach to completing tasks in a sequential manner. Attempting to undertake all of them simultaneously may result in an excessive amount of modification as the body and mind do not adapt in such a manner.

I have incorporated numerous efficacious fitness practices into my routine, one of which holds significant personal significance. Approximately one year ago, I became cognizant of a significant issue affecting my ocular health. The severity of the condition escalated to such an extent that I harbored concerns of losing my vision, which had an alarming effect on me. My profession entails writing as a means of sustenance. I allocate the major portion of my time towards working on the computer, and I began to experience anxiety contemplating on the possibility of being visually impaired which could impede my ability to provide for my family. My daughter and son rely on me;

that's a great weight I carry on my shoulders.

During the course of my investigative efforts, I have come to the conclusion that no visual impairment is present in my eyes. I seem to be experiencing ocular issues while operating a computer. Regrettably, I am unable to dedicate twelve hours of my day to a computer, as I once did when I pursued a writing career. I'm a big writer. Having authored a plethora of books and ghostwritten over a hundred for various clients, the thought of losing my utmost ability instilled great fear within me.

Through the course of the aforementioned progression, I gained the realization that I must procure a sustainable means for providing ongoing financial support for my family in the event of visual impairment. Accordingly, I embarked upon a series of trials involving various methods and technologies, ultimately modifying my strategy. Presently, I compose all of my literary works through dictation. I am consistently exploring diverse approaches to enhance my efficiency and generate content seamlessly, without necessitating direct interaction with a computer.

During the inception of my dictation practice, I used to take a seat in proximity to my beachfront residence at a local restaurant prior to commencing dictation. I would perceive the undulations of the ocean, peruse my framework, and verbalize succinctly. I subsequently transitioned and established a novel behavioral pattern. Whilst speaking, I am traversing a quay of thirty feet in length, steadily pacing back and forth over the rippling waters. See what I did? I have discovered a method of incorporating an additional healthy practice. Rather than confining myself to a computer for twelve hours per day, I engage in a three to four hour walk which permits me to accomplish an equivalent volume of work.

It consumed considerable time for me to construct this process; however, the integration of several habits enabled me to successfully accomplish it. It is imperative that you refrain from attempting to rectify or alter numerous habits concurrently, as it may lead to an ineffective outcome. Alternatively, it is advisable to address one habit at a time to achieve gradual personal improvement. This approach ensures a manageable and non-stressful process that guarantees continuous growth.

Ultimately, refraining from smoking or adopting any practice solely due to external pressure is an ineffective strategy. It's not enough motivation. Regrettably, acquiring detrimental habits through this means is relatively effortless, yet obtaining constructive habits is considerably arduous.

Steve has recently distributed a comprehensive questionnaire to his entire audience. He inquired: What was the primary obstacle hindering your attempt to cease smoking? What was your greatest success? May I inquire about the methodologies you have employed in your previous endeavors? Our objective was to establish a connection with our readership and ensure that this book accurately reflects upon the individual experiences of each individual.

An observation that came to our attention was that a number of individuals acknowledged the necessity to relinquish their current behavior but are experiencing an unwillingness to do so. And that's OK. It could be possible that you are not presently in a state where you are inclined to discontinue, and unless you adopt a compelling reason, you may not possess the urge to do so, and consequently will not take concrete actions towards it. None of us engage in activities that do not align with our intrinsic motivations, despite recognizing their importance. It is a widely acknowledged fact that maintaining a consistent consumption pattern of nutritious and wholesome foods on a daily basis is ideal, but regrettably, such a lifestyle is seldom practiced.

Allow us to assist you in discovering your fundamental purpose and motivation.

We have previously discussed a multitude of factors that motivate individuals to discontinue their engagement and the diverse advantages associated with such an action. However, I would like to urge you to elucidate further on this matter with explicit details. If you are able to articulate your motivation with a high degree of specificity, you will foster a deeper connection to it.

The statement "I want to maintain good health" holds lesser impact when compared to "I aim to avoid succumbing to emphysema like my late uncle," or "I intend to prevent using a COPD device that hinders my breathing at night, which may lead to my son fearing me, and ultimately avoiding sharing a room with me."

My fundamental motivation was rooted in the desire to ensure that my daughter would not be left alone in this world prematurely in the event of my untimely demise. It is of utmost importance to me that not even a single day is lost in the company of my partner. Therefore, despite the fact that I am currently dictating this book from my dockside, I am pleased to note that my beloved is engaging in kickboxing training with our instructor, a mere fifty yards away, and that she is well within the reach of my sight. The significance of my personal motive cannot be overstated.

There exist numerous reasons that may be compatible with your circumstances. May I suggest a formalized version of the same sentence, "Considering the amount of money I spend annually on smoking, I intend to channel those funds towards purchasing a new car or taking a vacation of my choice instead. It would be prudent to set a particular goal and start saving towards it."

Reflection Questions

Kindly examine each distinct class of advantages associated with smoking cessation and identify the ones that strongly correspond with your personal preferences.

After determining the categories that evoke the strongest resonance within oneself, categorize and prioritize them based on their duration and level of emotional attachment.

Please articulate precise and detailed declarations for each classification, for instance, 'My desire is to not perish at a premature age', or 'I harbor trepidations with regards to contracting lung cancer', or 'It is my utmost intention to ensure that my child never has to inquire whether my life is in peril.'

Proceed with this methodology of addressing the posed inquiries consistently, until arriving at the underlying motive or reason for your actions. The response that shall have the most profound impact on your being is the one that resonates with you on a visceral level, evoking a sensation that strikes at the very core of your being, compelling tears to well up within you as you pen it down. At that juncture, you have discovered the underlying cause for your actions.

Your Action Plan

Persist in addressing these reflection prompts and endeavor to ascertain the underlying motivation that defines your ultimate purpose. As an integral step in this procedure, we recommend that you contemplate becoming a member of a community or our Facebook group and posting inquiries regarding your personal encounters. Engagement in this process need not be undertaken in isolation. Your prescribed task is to locate and become a member of a community, wherein you may proffer the reasons underlying your participation.

If you have not yet established the central motivation driving your actions, you may engage in relevant inquiries within the group, peruse other individuals' motivations, and leverage the communal resources to discover your own. After dissemination amidst our community, kindly transcribe it within your journal and subsequently incorporate it into your vision board.

It is advisable to document your objective and give it a tangible representation. Actualize your conceptualization and transfer it onto a tangible medium. After establishing a connection with our esteemed community and crafting an impactful visualization, kindly proceed to Step 2 and accompany me in the forthcoming chapter.

www.ingramcontent.com/pod-product-compliance
Lightning Source LLC
Chambersburg PA
CBHW050028130526
44590CB00042B/2043